A Mighty

WARRIOR'S

Journal of Healing and Strength

For those who have battled cancer – a space for reflection, healing, and empowerment.

A Healing Journal for
Survivors
By Kimani

This journal is dedicated to my fellow Survivor Sisters and Brothers, who have faced the challenges of cancer with bravery and resilience.

May this guide help you reflect, heal, and discover the strength within to thrive.

WITH LOVE,
Kimani

Greetings, My Survivor Sisters and Brothers!

As you know better than anyone, fighting cancer is a traumatic experience for all involved, especially the patients. It is an experience filled with a range of emotions: fear, resentment, insecurity, anxiety, and more. Unfortunately, many of us rarely take the time to sit with these emotions and process them fully.

While the cancer experience is undeniably traumatic, it is also transformative. It can transform us either negatively or positively, but ultimately, it is up to us to decide how we will survive, thrive, and triumph.

To assist you in your journey, I have arranged prompts to provide a space for you to reflect, heal, and empower yourself through your independent process.

I want to support my survivor sisters and brothers in processing their experiences and finding strength in their journey, as the superheroes you truly are!

With love,
Kimani

- **Pacing Yourself**
  Consider using one prompt per day or per week, depending on your comfort level and available time. Consistent journaling can be therapeutic.

- **Create a Safe Space**
  Create a comfortable, private environment for your journaling sessions where you feel free to express yourself openly.

- **No "Right" Way**
  Remember, there is no "right" way to respond to these prompts. Write as much or as little as you feel comfortable with.

- **Listen to Your Emotions**
  Pay attention to your emotions as you write. If a prompt brings up difficult feelings, it's okay to take a break or switch to a different prompt.

- **Review and Reflect**
  After some time, go back and read your earlier entries. This can help you see how far you've come and how your perspectives may have changed.

- **Share with Care**
  If you feel comfortable, consider sharing some of your reflections with trusted friends, family, or a support group. This can foster connection and understanding. Choose with whom you share wisely.

- **Engage with Support**
  These prompts can also be topics for discussions with your care team, therapist, or support group.

- **Personalize the Prompts**
  Feel free to modify the prompts or create your own based on what feels most relevant to your journey.

Today's Date : _____

Describe the moment you first received your diagnosis.

What was the date? Where were you? Who was with you?
Who did you tell first?
What emotions did you experience?
How did you cope with them?

_____

_____

_____

_____

_____

_____

_____

_____

_____

_____

_____

_____

_____

_____

_____

_____

_____

_____

_____

"I am not only a casualty, I am also a warrior."
- Audre Lorde

Today's Date : _____

Reflect and write about the most challenging part of your journey so far.

How have you overcome it?

_____
_____
_____
_____
_____
_____
_____
_____
_____
_____
_____
_____
_____
_____
_____
_____
_____
_____
_____
_____

"I am not only a casualty, I am also a warrior."
- Audre Lorde

Share the lesson(s) you have learned about life, relationships, yourself, etc.

_____
_____
_____
_____
_____
_____
_____
_____
_____
_____
_____
_____
_____
_____
_____
_____
_____
_____
_____

Quote: "I am not only a casualty, I am also a warrior."
- Audre Lorde

Today's Date : _____

Reflect on a moment when you felt overwhelmed.

How did you get through it?

_____
_____
_____
_____
_____
_____
_____
_____
_____
_____
_____
_____
_____
_____
_____
_____
_____

"Life provides losses and heartbreak for all of us, but the greatest tragedy is to have the experience and miss the meaning." - Robin Roberts

Today's Date : _____

Describe the moment you first received your diagnosis.

How do you cope with fear of recurrence or uncertainty about the future?
Explore ways to cope with these fears and list them.
(Ask other survivors, Google, Siri, a medical/therapeutic professional, etc.)

_____
_____
_____
_____
_____
_____
_____
_____
_____
_____
_____
_____
_____
_____
_____
_____
_____
_____

"Life provides losses and heartbreak for all of us, but the greatest tragedy is to have the experience and miss the meaning." – Robin Roberts

KNOTED
By Kimani

Detail aspects of your treatment that have surprised you, either positively or negatively.

_____
_____
_____
_____
_____
_____
_____
_____
_____
_____
_____
_____
_____
_____
_____
_____
_____
_____
_____
_____

"Life provides losses and heartbreak for all of us, but the greatest tragedy is to have the experience and miss the meaning." – Robin Roberts

KNOTED
By Kimani

Describe your "new normal".

How does it differ from your life before cancer?
Do people treat you differently (better or worse)?

_____
_____
_____
_____
_____
_____
_____
_____
_____
_____
_____
_____
_____
_____
_____
_____
_____

**"You may encounter many defeats,
but you must not be defeated. In fact, it may be
necessary to encounter the defeats, so you can know
who you are, what you can rise from, how you
can still come out of it." - Maya Angelou**

Today's Date : _____

Convey your thoughts about how your relationship with your body changed throughout this journey.

Do you have any body image insecurities (scars, mastectomy, weight loss/gain, etc.)?
Why are you insecure about this part of your body?
Has your relationship with your body improved in any way?
Explore and list possible ways to overcome your insecurities and/or to help someone overcome theirs. (Ask other survivors, Google, Siri, a medical/therapeutic professional, etc.)

_____
_____
_____
_____
_____
_____
_____
_____
_____
_____
_____
_____
_____

"You may encounter many defeats, but you must not be defeated. In fact, it may be necessary to encounter the defeats, so you can know who you are, what you can rise from, how you can still come out of it." - Maya Angelou

Today's Date : _____

List three things you are grateful for today.

How do these things bring joy or comfort to your life?

"Every day is a winding road, but I'm
learning to enjoy the journey." – Sheryl Crow

KNOTED
By Kimani

Write about a person who has been a
source of support for you.

How have they impacted your journey?

_____
_____
_____
_____
_____
_____
_____
_____
_____
_____
_____
_____
_____
_____
_____
_____
_____
_____
_____

**"Every day is a winding road, but I'm
learning to enjoy the journey." - Sheryl Crow**

Reflect and write about the most rewarding part of your journey so far.

How has it enriched you/your life?

_____
_____
_____
_____
_____
_____
_____
_____
_____
_____
_____
_____
_____
_____
_____
_____
_____
_____

"Every day is a winding road, but I'm learning to enjoy the journey." – Sheryl Crow

Detail some self-care practices that help you feel more at peace.

How can you incorporate them into your daily routine?

_____
_____
_____
_____
_____
_____
_____
_____
_____
_____
_____
_____
_____
_____
_____
_____
_____
_____

"A really strong woman accepts the war she went through and is ennobled by her scars." - Carly Simon

Today's Date : _____

Recount a moment when you felt truly at ease or happy during your treatment.

What made that moment special?

_____
_____
_____
_____
_____
_____
_____
_____
_____
_____
_____
_____
_____
_____
_____
_____
_____
_____
_____
_____

"A really strong woman accepts the war she went through and is ennobled by her scars." - Carly Simon

Write a letter to a loved one you feel "let you down" during treatment.

Writing with the intention to forgive and heal is encouraged but not necessary at this time. Expressing your true, raw feelings is the priority and purpose.

"A really strong woman accepts the war she went through and is ennobled by her scars." - Carly Simon

KNOTED
By Kimani

Today's Date: _____

Illustrate (in writing) your hopes and dreams for the future.

How has your experience with breast cancer shaped these aspirations?

_____

_____

_____

_____

_____

_____

_____

_____

_____

_____

_____

_____

_____

_____

_____

_____

_____

_____

"Once I overcame breast cancer, I wasn't afraid of anything anymore." - Melissa Etheridge

Today's Date: _____

Imagine yourself five years from now.

What do you see, and how do you feel?

_____

_____

_____

_____

_____

_____

_____

_____

_____

_____

_____

_____

_____

_____

_____

_____

_____

_____

_____

"Once I overcame breast cancer, I wasn't afraid of anything anymore." - Melissa Etheridge

Today's Date: _____

Share how your sense of purpose or life goals have shifted since your diagnosis.

_____
_____
_____
_____
_____
_____
_____
_____
_____
_____
_____
_____
_____
_____
_____
_____
_____
_____
_____

"Once I overcame breast cancer, I wasn't afraid of anything anymore." - Melissa Etheridge

Today's Date: _____

List some positive changes you'd like to make in your life moving forward.

_____

_____

_____

_____

_____

_____

_____

_____

_____

_____

_____

_____

_____

_____

_____

_____

_____

_____

_____

"You were given this life because you are strong enough to live it." - Unknown

KNOTED
By Kimani

Chronicle the milestones in your cancer journey.

How do you plan to celebrate them?

_____
_____
_____
_____
_____
_____
_____
_____
_____
_____
_____
_____
_____
_____
_____
_____
_____
_____
_____
_____
_____
_____

"You were given this life because you are strong enough to live it." – Unknown

Today's Date : _____

Compose a letter to your pre-cancer self.

What would you want yourself to know (warning, advice, etc.)?

_____
_____
_____
_____
_____
_____
_____
_____
_____
_____
_____
_____
_____
_____
_____
_____
_____
_____
_____
_____
_____

"Life is not about waiting for the storms to pass. It's about learning how to dance in the rain." - Vivian Greene

Today's Date : _____

Write about a time when you felt strong and empowered during your journey.

What contributed to that feeling?

_____
_____
_____
_____
_____
_____
_____
_____
_____
_____
_____
_____
_____
_____
_____
_____
_____
_____
_____
_____
_____

"Life is not about waiting for the storms to pass. It's about learning how to dance in the rain." - Vivian Greene

Today's Date : _____

Capture about what "survivorship" means to you.

"Life is not about waiting for the storms to pass. It's about learning how to dance in the rain." - Vivian Greene

Today's Date: _____

Reflect on the strength of the breast cancer community.

If you have connected with a breast cancer community, how has it impacted your journey?
If you have not connected with a community, research some and list them with contact information.

"Courage doesn't always roar. Sometimes courage is the quiet voice at the end of the day saying, 'I will try again tomorrow.'" – Mary Anne Radmacher

Today's Date: _____

Share advice for someone newly diagnosed with breast cancer.

Consider what you wish you had known before treatment regarding medication, surgeries, medical procedures, support systems, resources, etc.

_____
_____
_____
_____
_____
_____
_____
_____
_____
_____
_____
_____
_____
_____
_____
_____
_____
_____

"Courage doesn't always roar. Sometimes courage is the quiet voice at the end of the day saying, 'I will try again tomorrow.'" – Mary Anne Radmacher

Today's Date: _____

Write an open message to others, letting them know what you want them to understand about your experience with breast cancer.

_____
_____
_____
_____
_____
_____
_____
_____
_____
_____
_____
_____
_____
_____
_____
_____
_____
_____
_____

"Cancer may have started the fight, but I will finish it." - Unknown

Create a poem or a short story that reflects
your journey.

Use figurative language (similes, metaphors, etc.) or imagery that resonate with your experience.

_____
_____
_____
_____
_____
_____
_____
_____
_____
_____
_____
_____
_____
_____
_____
_____
_____
_____
_____

**"Cancer may have started the fight,
but I will finish it." - Unknown**

Today's Date: _____

Create or describe a symbol that represents your strength and resilience.

_____
_____
_____
_____
_____
_____
_____
_____
_____
_____
_____
_____
_____
_____
_____
_____
_____
_____
_____

"Cancer may have started the fight, but I will finish it." - Unknown

Remember, there are no right or wrong answers. These prompts are meant to help you explore your thoughts and feelings at your own pace. Writing can be a powerful tool for healing and self-discovery. If at any point you feel overwhelmed, it's okay to take a break or seek support from a mental health professional.

As a fellow breast cancer survivor, I understand the journey and the strength it takes to navigate through it. I am here to offer my unwavering support and solidarity to all survivors.

In addition to my personal support, I bring my professional expertise through my editing and writing business, kNotED by Kimani. Whether you need assistance in crafting your story, refining your words, or simply want to connect with someone who understands, I am available to help.

Together, we can elevate your voice and share your unique journey with the world. Reach out to me at kimani@knoted.net or www.knoted-by-kimani.com, and let's create something beautiful together!

With love,
Kimani

www.ingramcontent.com/pod-product-compliance
Lightning Source LLC
Chambersburg PA
CBHW051647120626
46551CB00015B/2257